Dear Parents and Educators,

Welcome to Penguin Young Readers! As parents and educators, you know that each child develops at his or her own pace—in terms of speech, critical thinking, and, of course, reading. Penguin Young Readers recognizes this fact. As a result, each Penguin Young Readers book is assigned a traditional easy-to-read level (1–4) as well as a Guided Reading Level (A–P). Both of these systems will help you choose the right book for your child. Please refer to the back of each book for specific leveling information. Penguin Young Readers features esteemed authors and illustrators, stories about favorite characters, fascinating nonfiction, and more!

Turtles

LEVEL 2

GUIDED READING LEVEL **F**

This book is perfect for a **Progressing Reader** who:
- can figure out unknown words by using picture and context clues;
- can recognize beginning, middle, and ending sounds;
- can make and confirm predictions about what will happen in the text; and
- can distinguish between fiction and nonfiction.

Here are some **activities** you can do during and after reading this book:
- This book is nonfiction. Nonfiction books deal with facts and events that are real. Talk about the elements of nonfiction books. Then discuss what you learned in this book. For example, some turtles can live for 70 or 80 years. See how many facts about turtles you can find!
- Compare/Contrast: Some turtles live in the sea and are called sea turtles. Others live on land and are usually called tortoises. How are sea turtles and tortoises alike? How are they different? Use a separate sheet of paper to make a list.

Remember, sharing the love of reading with a child is the best gift you can give!

—Bonnie Bader, EdM
  Penguin Young Readers program

*Penguin Young Readers are leveled by independent reviewers applying the standards developed by Irene Fountas and Gay Su Pinnell in *Matching Books to Readers: Using Leveled Books in Guided Reading*, Heinemann, 1999.

For my Pop-Pop, in loving memory—JH

In memory of Emilio and
Carmelina González Trujillo—PJG

Penguin Young Readers
Published by the Penguin Group
Penguin Group (USA) Inc., 375 Hudson Street, New York, New York 10014, USA
Penguin Group (Canada), 90 Eglinton Avenue East, Suite 700, Toronto, Ontario M4P 2Y3, Canada
(a division of Pearson Penguin Canada Inc.)
Penguin Books Ltd., 80 Strand, London WC2R 0RL, England
Penguin Group Ireland, 25 St. Stephen's Green, Dublin 2, Ireland (a division of Penguin Books Ltd.)
Penguin Group (Australia), 250 Camberwell Road, Camberwell, Victoria 3124, Australia
(a division of Pearson Australia Group Pty. Ltd.)
Penguin Books India Pvt. Ltd., 11 Community Centre, Panchsheel Park, New Delhi—110 017, India
Penguin Group (NZ), 67 Apollo Drive, Rosedale, Auckland 0632, New Zealand
(a division of Pearson New Zealand Ltd.)
Penguin Books (South Africa) (Pty.) Ltd., 24 Sturdee Avenue,
Rosebank, Johannesburg 2196, South Africa

Penguin Books Ltd., Registered Offices: 80 Strand, London WC2R 0RL, England

Library of Congress Control Number: 2002151239

ISBN 978-0-448-43117-8   10 9 8 7 6 5 4

Turtles

by Jodi Huelin
illustrated by Pedro Julio González

Penguin Young Readers
An Imprint of Penguin Group (USA) Inc.

ook over there—

in the water.

Do you see a turtle?

LOGGERHEAD TURTLE

LOGGERHEAD TURTLE

It is a sea turtle.

It has long, strong flippers.

They help the turtle to swim.

Sea turtles are

almost always swimming.

7

This sea turtle

has come on land.

She is ready to lay her eggs!

LOGGERHEAD TURTLE

She lays her eggs at night.

She lays them in holes.

Then she goes back to the water.

9

Two months pass.

The eggs hatch one by one.

After three days,

the baby turtles head

for the water.

GREEN TURTLE
HATCHLINGS

Only a few will make it.

Baby turtles are a tasty snack

for birds and animals.

LEATHERBACK TURTLE

If the baby turtles
reach the water,
they start swimming
right away.

12

Sea turtles are good swimmers.

Sea turtles are good divers, too.

Some like to dive for jellyfish.

Different sea turtles

eat different things.

Some eat plants.

Like sea grass and seaweed.

GREEN TURTLE

OLIVE RIDLEY

Others eat small creatures.

Like clams and shrimp.

15

EASTERN RIVER
COOTER

Turtles need soft food—

they don't have teeth!

They do have **very** strong jaws.

Turtles also have beaks.

The beaks help them tear food.

Even though turtles

don't have teeth,

they can still bite.

SNAPPING TURTLE

BOX TURTLE

Some turtles live on land.

They are usually called tortoises.

They do not swim.

They only go to the water

to drink and take baths.

You can visit turtles at the zoo.

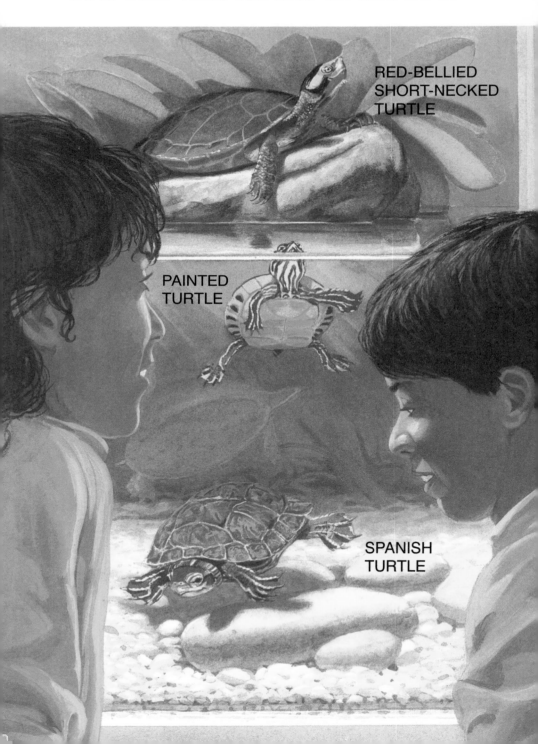

RED-BELLIED
SHORT-NECKED
TURTLE

PAINTED
TURTLE

SPANISH
TURTLE

You can keep some kinds
of turtles as pets.

BABY
PAINTED
TURTLE

Always wash your hands
after you touch a turtle.

Sea turtles and land turtles
can live indoors in a fish tank.
Land turtles can also live
outside in a pen.

TORTOISE

You can feed them salad
and flowers and fruits
and vegetables.

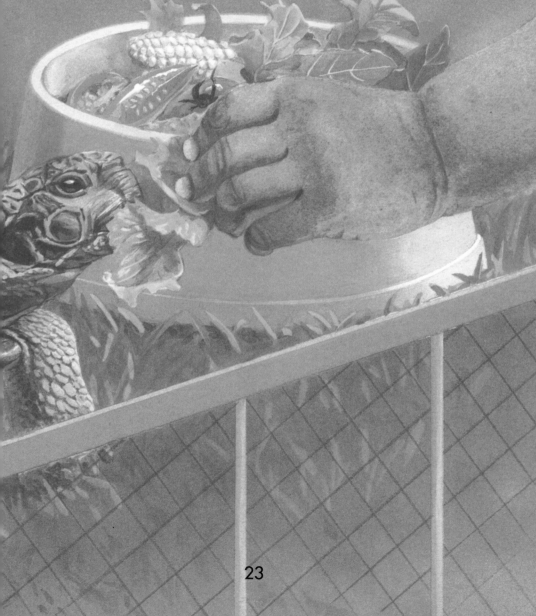

Some turtles live

a pretty long time.

Like 30 or 40 years.

PAINTED TURTLE

Other turtles live

a **really** long time.

Like 70 or 80 years.

GIANT
GALAPAGOS
TORTOISE

CAR

LEATHERBACK TURTLE

BOG TURTLE

Some turtles are

a few inches long.

LEATHERBACK TURTLE

BOG TURTLE

But some are over six feet long.

That's almost as long as a car!

DESERT TORTOISE

Most turtles have soft bodies
and hard shells.

The shell protects the turtle.

It keeps the turtle's body safe.

Land turtles can tuck

their heads and legs

in their shells

if there is danger.

Sea turtles can't do this.

DESERT TORTOISE

GREEN TURTLE

So what do sea turtles do

if there is danger?

They swim away, of course!